WORLD'S WORST...

SPACE Disasters

Rob Alcraft

Heinemann
LIBRARY

First published in Great Britain by Heinemann Library,
Halley Court, Jordan Hill, Oxford OX2 8EJ
a division of Reed Educational and Professional Publishing Ltd.

Heinemann is a registered trademark of Reed Educational & Professional Publishing Ltd.

OXFORD MELBOURNE AUCKLAND
JOHANNESBURG BLANTYRE GABORONE
IBADAN PORTSMOUTH (NH) USA CHICAGO

Designed by Celia Floyd
Illustrations by David Cuzik (Pennant Illustration)
Originated by Dot Gradations, UK
Printed by Wing King Tong, in Hong Kong

04 03 02 01 00
10 9 8 7 6 5 4 3 2 1

ISBN 0 431 01287 3

British Library Cataloguing in Publication Data

Alcraft, Rob, 1966–
World's worst space disasters
1. Space vehicle accidents – Juvenile literature
I. Title II. Space disasters
363.1'24

Acknowledgements

The Publishers would like to thank the following for permission to reproduce photographs:
Image Select: p.4, p.21; Novosti (London): p.14, p.15, p.18, p.19, p.29; Planet Earth Pictures: p.7, p.8, p.24, p.25, NASA p.12; Science Photo Library: Mark Paternostro p.28, NASA p.9, p.13, p.20, p.27, Novosti p.5; Tony Stone: IM House p.26, NASA p.6.

Cover photograph reproduced with permission of NASA: Science Photo Library

Our thanks to Dr Henry Wilson of the International Journal of Disaster Prevention and Management, Department of Industrial Technology, University of Bradford for his comments in the preparation of this book.

For more information about Heinemann Library books, or to order, please telephone +44 (0)1865 888066, or send a fax to +44 (0)1865 314091. You can visit our website at www.heinemann.co.uk

Any words appearing in the text in bold, **like this**, are explained in the Glossary.

RESOURCE CENTRE

WESTERN ISLES LIBRARIES

Readers are requested to take great care of the books while in their possession, and to point out any defects that they may notice in them to the Librarian.
This book is issued for a period of twenty-one days and should be returned on or before the latest date stamped below, but an extension of the period of loan may be granted when desired.

DATE OF RETURN	DATE OF RETURN	DATE OF RETURN
1 5 APR 2015		
3 0 SEP 2020		
3 0 SEP 2020		

WITHDRAWN

Contents

The Journey into Space

Space travel has become part of our lives. We take it for granted. Today **satellites** and rockets are launched almost as a matter of routine. Perhaps we have forgotten how amazing and dangerous space travel really is. Within the life-time of your grandparents, it was thought that space travel was an impossible dream. Even if we could get a human into space, no-one was sure what would happen to them when they got there.

James Irwin, from the *Apollo 15* mission stands on the moon's surface and salutes the US flag.

In 1961 the **Soviet Union** launched the *Vostok 1*. Inside was Yuri Gagarin, the first person in space. He made one complete **orbit** round the Earth. Despite fears about what would happen to him, he landed safely. Within three years the first **space walk** was safely completed. Four years later, in 1969, the American *Apollo 7* mission landed Neil Armstrong and Edwin 'Buzz' Aldrin on the Moon. It seemed to many people that space had been conquered. But the risks remained.

Alongside the success stories, there have also been disasters. In this book we look at three of the worst disasters in the history of space exploration. Minute by minute we look at what went wrong. We look at the technology and the dangers of space travel. What could have been done to prevent disaster? Who, if anyone, was to blame?

The first living thing in space was a Russian dog called Laika. She was sent up in a **pressurized** cabin in *Sputnik 2*. Laika spent a week in space before scientists on the ground put her to sleep by remote control.

Animals in space

The first test pilots for manned space flight were monkeys and dogs. In the 1950s both Russia and America used them to test the effects of space on living things – and to see how safe the early rockets and spacecraft really were. The first living thing from Earth to make it into space was a dog called Laika. Laika blasted off into space aboard the Russian *Sputnik 2* on 3 November 1957.

Reaching for the Stars

Space is a dangerous place to go. Even getting there is dangerous. Space rockets are really no more than huge fireworks which can, if things go wrong, explode.

Ordinary jet engines are not powerful enough to produce the huge thrust a spacecraft needs to escape Earth's **gravity**. Instead a space rocket burns oxygen and hydrogen. Both gases are extremely explosive, and many rockets – fortunately few of them carrying people – have not even made it off the **launch pad**. Their fuel tanks have simply exploded.

When a space rocket reaches space there are further dangers. Space is a **vacuum**. There is no air and it is very, very cold. A spacecraft must carry everything astronauts need to survive – including the air they need to breathe! Spacecrafts must be completely sealed off from the outside – even a tiny leak of air alters the **air pressure** and the astronauts inside die.

This is what the earth looks like from space. Pictures like this are familiar today, but before space travel no-one had ever seen what the Earth looked like.

Dangers and risks

After lift-off the next most dangerous part of the journey into space is **re-entry** when the spacecraft plunges back into the Earth's **atmosphere**. Often the **friction** between the spacecraft and the atmosphere makes temperatures soar to more than 1600°C (2912°F). Old **satellites** and **meteorites** burn up in the atmosphere before they reach the ground. A spacecraft needs to get through intact if its crew are to survive.

There have been more than 207 manned missions into space. Given the risks it is amazing that so few have ended in disaster. There is no room for even the smallest error in space travel. Even small mistakes can bring tragic results.

Lift-off!

The European *Ariane* rocket is 57m high and can lift a load of 4 tonnes into an **orbit** 400km above the Earth. *Ariane* – like most rocket systems – uses three stages to escape Earth's gravity.

1 Lift-off, and the powerful liquid-fuel engines and **booster rockets** light. At 60km up, the booster rockets run out of fuel. They separate and float to Earth by parachute.

2 Next the main engine fires and burns. This engine then falls away, and burns up on re-entry.

3 The final-stage rocket fires, propelling *Ariane* to around 28,800km per hour, fast enough to leave the Earth's atmosphere, and into the planned orbit.

Ariane 4 took off on its first flight in June 1988. It was carrying satellites.

Explosion!
Near Disaster for Apollo 13

Apollo 13 took off on 11 April 1970. The mission of the three astronauts inside, John L. Swigert, Fred W. Haise Jr. and Captain James Lovell, was to land on the Moon. But they never got there. On 13 April an explosion on board left the men fighting for survival.

A good start

At 1.13pm on 11 April 1970 *Apollo 13* was launched. It had three different rocket stages, and after each stage did its job it was **jettisoned**. Three more stages entered space. The **Service Module** was packed with equipment. The **Command Module** (*Odyssey*) was the astronauts' home for the journey. The **Lunar Module** (*Aquarius*) was to take two men down to the Moon.

46 hours into the flight the commander on duty at the Kennedy Space Centre in Houston, Texas, joked to the astronauts: 'The spacecraft is in real good shape as far as we are concerned. We're bored to tears down here.' There was even time for a TV broadcast from the crew showing life in the **weightless** conditions of space.

Initially all appears to be going well as *Apollo 13*, powered by a *Saturn V* rocket, blasts off for its journey to the moon.

Emergency in space

Captain James Lovell from the *Apollo 13* mission, during training.

Then, after just 56 hours in space, oxygen tank number two suddenly exploded. Tank one also failed. Inside the Command Module warning lights flashed. Then, one after the other, all power, light and heat systems failed. The three astronauts were 320,000km from home and the oxygen supply in the Command Module was running out. If something was not done soon, the astronauts would die.

Captain James Lovell, speaking after the event:

'When you first hear this explosion or bang...you don't know what it is. Then I looked out of the window and saw this **venting**. My concern was increasing all the time. I went from 'I wonder what this is going to do to the landing' to 'I wonder if we can get back home again' and when I looked up and saw both oxygen pressures...one actually at zero and the other one going down... it dawned on me that we were in serious trouble.'

"Houston, we have a problem"

Deep in space in *Apollo 13*. Lovell peered out of the window. He could see a thin cloud of gas boiling out into space. It was making the spacecraft spin wildly. *Apollo 13* was in serious trouble.

1   On April 13, 1970, at 55 hours and 55 minutes into the *Apollo 13* mission, an oxygen tank explodes. A second tank is damaged and its oxygen lost. The craft's **fuel cells** need oxygen to work, so these begin to fail.

2   On Earth experts realize it is too dangerous to use the main engine on the **Service Module**. But the smaller engine on the **Lunar Module** does not have enough power to turn *Apollo* around. The only option is to use the **gravitational pull** of the Moon to 'swing' *Apollo 13* back towards Earth.

3   An hour later the crew of *Apollo 13* decided to abandon the **Command Module** because it only has enough power and oxygen left to last through **re-entry**. They enter the Lunar Module. This is designed to keep two men alive for 45 hours. Now it must keep three men alive for 84 hours. To survive, they build a makeshift air filter to allow them to breathe for the extra hours.

4   Mission Control decides to try two burns of the Lunar Module engine – one to put *Apollo 13* on the right course and a second to speed it on its way. 60 hours into the mission the crew do the first engine burn for 35 seconds.

5   Almost 76½ hours into the mission *Apollo 13* passes behind the Moon. For 25 minutes it is out of radio contact with Earth. The crew make a second engine burn for five minutes, but *Apollo 13* drifts off course. At 128 hours and 31 minutes into the mission the descent engine is fired to slow the craft down, and to make sure it hits the Earth's atmosphere at the right angle.

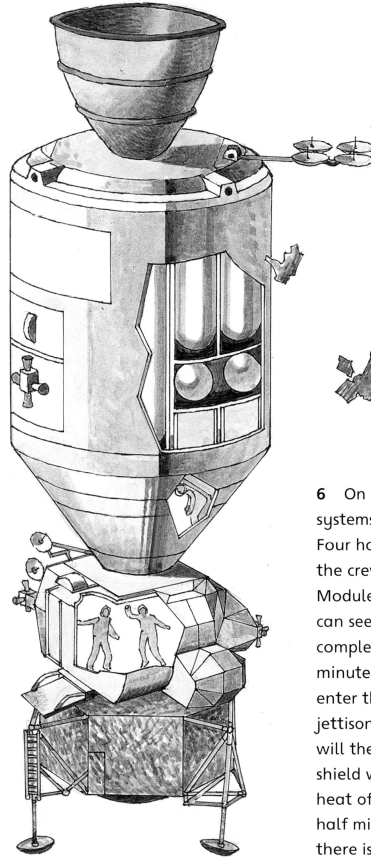

6 On 17 April Lunar Module systems are switched on again. Four hours before splash-down the crew **jettison** the Service Module. As it drifts away they can see that one side had been completely blown off. At 90 minutes before re-entry, the crew enter the Command Module and jettison the Lunar Module. But will the Command Module's heat shield withstand the incredible heat of re-entry? For three and half minutes, during re-entry there is silence.

Splash Down

Apollo 13 made it home. The heat shield worked and the crew were alive. But what had gone wrong to cause this near disaster? The investigations that followed quickly showed how even small errors can lead to potentially big disasters.

Apollo 13 parachuted safely into the sea. The astronauts arrived home to a great welcome.

Engineer detectives

A team of **NASA** engineers tracked down the history of the defective oxygen tank and tested their theories on an identical tank. They discovered that while oxygen tank number two, which had exploded on the mission, was being made it had been damaged. They also found that when both tanks were redesigned the **thermostatic** switches, which controlled the temperature, were not changed.

Before the launch the oxygen tanks were tested. During this testing **Teflon** insulation on electrical wires inside tank number two were damaged. This damage went unnoticed until things started to go wrong on the mission. The faulty wires caused sparks and then an explosion. The fate of *Apollo 13* was sealed before it even left the ground.

Lessons learned

NASA's careful investigations led to a number of recommendations to improve safety on future spacecraft. These included the instruction that whenever even slight problems occur with systems before a launch, the history of that instrument or part should be carefully studied before it is allowed to be used.

They also decided that oxgyen storage systems should be altered to reduce the risk of fire, for example by minimizing the use of Teflon and other **combustible** materials. NASA also reviewed what foodstuffs and emergency equipment should be kept in the **Command Module** or other 'extra' modules, in case they are needed in an emergency.

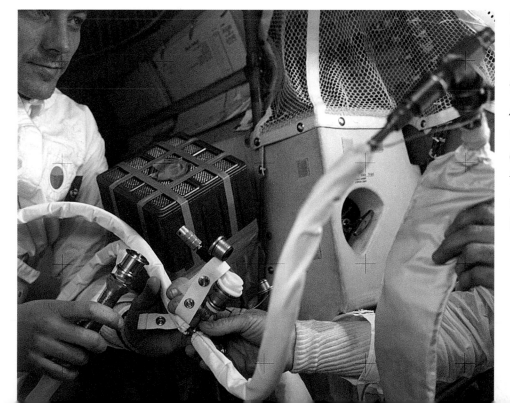

In order to breathe in the **Lunar Module** the crew of *Apollo 13* had to make an emergency air filter from materials on board.

Disaster!
The End of the Soyuz 11 Mission

On 29 June 1971 the **Command Module** of the **Soviet Union's** *Soyuz 11* spacecraft was recovered in Kazakhstan. A hero's welcome was planned. But inside the capsule, the crew were dead.

The longest mission

The Soviet Union launched the world's first space station, called *Salyut 1*, on 19 April 1971. It was a floating laboratory. On board were more than 1300 scientific instruments, including a tiny 'farm' for plant experiments.

Soyuz 11 was designed to ferry scientists up to the space station. It was launched on the morning of 6 June 1971. At first it seemed a total success. The three **cosmonauts** on board *Soyuz 11* boarded the space station without problems. For 22 days the crew completed scientific experiments. They studied the surface of Earth and its weather and cloud formations. The cosmonauts studied their own bodies, and how they reacted to the **weightlessness** of space.

A successful launch for *Soyuz 11*, on a mission to the *Salyut 1* space station. The three cosmonauts on board were to die 23 days later on **re-entry**.

On 24 June they had beaten the record for the longest ever space flight. Television pictures of the crew on board *Soyuz 11* were beamed across the Soviet Union. They become national heroes as they somersaulted across the screens of millions of viewers on Earth. Yet when they returned they were unable to enjoy the hero's welcome prepared for them. On 29 June 1971, as *Soyuz 11* re-entered the Earth's **atmosphere**, the three men died.

Penguin suits

Because there is no **gravity** in space many of the muscles that are essential on Earth grow weak and flabby. The three cosmonauts on *Soyuz 11* wore special elastic suits nick-named 'penguin suits'. The suits made the men work hard to move their muscles – it was a bit like they were constantly doing weight-lifting.

Viktor Patsayev
Profession: engineer
Born: 19-6-33
Missions flown: 1

Georgi Dobrovolsky (Commander)
Profession: pilot
Born: 1-6-28
Missions flown: 1

Vladislav Volkov
Profession: engineer
Born: 23-11-35
Missions flown: 2

No Hero's Welcome

When the deaths of the three **cosmonauts** were announced, world leaders and space experts sent messages to the **Soviet Union** expressing their sadness. George Low, the deputy director of **NASA**, said 'Our hearts go out to their families and to their colleagues.' Everyone wanted to know what had happened.

1   The *Soyuz 11* mission begins on 6 June 1971. *Soyuz 11* enters **orbit** nine minutes after launch. At 10:50 **GMT** it is circling 217km above the Earth. At this orbit it approaches the *Salyut 1* space station. On 7 June at 07:24 docking begins. The ship steers automatically until it is within 100m of the space station, and then Dobrovolsky takes the controls for docking. Later that day the crew enter the space station.

2   On 29 June, the crew of *Soyuz 11* close up the *Salyut 1* space station. At 18:28 GMT they set off for Earth. **Retro-fire** is complete at 22:35. 'This is Yantar 1,' says Dobrovolsky, giving his call sign, 'Everything is satisfactory on board. Our condition is excellent. We are ready to land.' Next the three parts of the *Soyuz 11* separate – explosive bolts sending the **Service Module** and **Orbital Module** away from the **Command Module**. There is no more radio contact.

3 The eerie silence is worrying. But the parachutes and rockets designed to give the cosmonauts a soft landing all work perfectly. The Command Module lands on target in Kazakhstan. Doctors are first on the scene to check the health of the three men. But when they open the capsule they find the three men hanging from the seat straps. Somehow, during the 20 minute **re-entry** phase of the mission, the three men have died.

4 An official announcement from the Soviet authorities says simply '...a helicopter-borne recovery group, upon opening the hatch, found the *Soyuz 11* crew in their seats without any signs of life. The causes of the crew's death are being investigated.'

The Missing Minutes

What had happened on board *Soyuz 11* between the last message from Commander Dobrovolsky and the silent landing in Kazakhstan? In Moscow, the capital of the **Soviet Union**, a special commission was set up to find out. Headed by Mstislav Keldysh, the President of the Soviet Union's Academy of Sciences, it began to talk to the experts responsible for the *Soyuz* mission.

Around the world experts on space travel tried to guess the cause of the disaster. Many thought that the heat shield that was meant to keep the **Command Module** cool as it plummeted back to Earth had failed. In Moscow people close to those who ran the *Soyuz* mission were saying that a hatch had not been closed. The air in the Command Module had leaked out, and the **cosmonauts** had died.

The *Soyuz 9* mission pictured here had a happy ending. However, when the *Soyuz 11* command module was opened up the deaths of the three crew members were discovered.

On 11 July 1971 Mstislav Keldysh gave the commission's findings. They said the disaster was due to '[a] rapid pressure drop occurring inside the descent vehicle.' Few other details were given because the Soviet authorities were secretive. They didn't want to give anyone else useful information, and they didn't like to admit mistakes in public.

It took two years before the full facts about *Soyuz 11* were made public. The disaster had been caused by the shock of the explosive bolts that separated the three stages of *Soyuz 11* just before **re-entry**. The bolts firing had caused a **valve** to open. The valve should not have opened until just before touch-down, to let air in. Instead, the valve had opened in space, and let all the air out, killing the crew.

No more short cuts

The most important lesson of the *Soyuz 11* disaster was that, when it came to space travel, nothing could be left to chance. The designers of the *Soyuz* craft thought that the cosmonauts did not need **pressure suits**. Anyway, inside the tiny Command Module there was not room for them to put them on. It was this short cut that killed the three men. When *Soyuz 12* was launched in 1973 it had only two men on board – so that there would be room for pressure suits.

The *Soyuz* disaster also spelled the end for the *Salyut 1* space station. With no safe way of sending men to work on it, it was steered back towards Earth and after 175 days in space it burnt up over the Pacific Ocean.

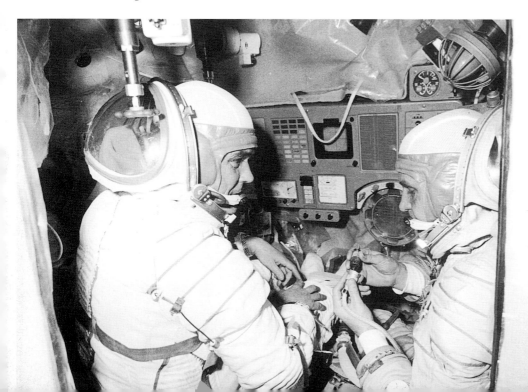

Important lessons were learned from *Soyuz 11*. The cosmonauts on board *Soyuz 12* were equipped with pressure suits.

Fireball!
The Challenger Space Shuttle Disaster

On 28 January 1986 an American Space Shuttle, *Challenger*, prepared for launch. Lift-off seemed to go well. But just 73 seconds after lift-off *Challenger* exploded in flames.

It was the twenty-fifth Shuttle mission. American astronauts had launched and returned safely 50 times in 25 years of space flight and exploration. Launches had become so routine that only one of America's TV networks was filming it. Yet on the ground at Cape Canaveral in Florida things were less than routine. Already there had been three launch postponements. Then on 27 January, as the astronauts were being strapped in for lift-off, a broken handle on a hatch, and then high winds, caused the launch to be called off again.

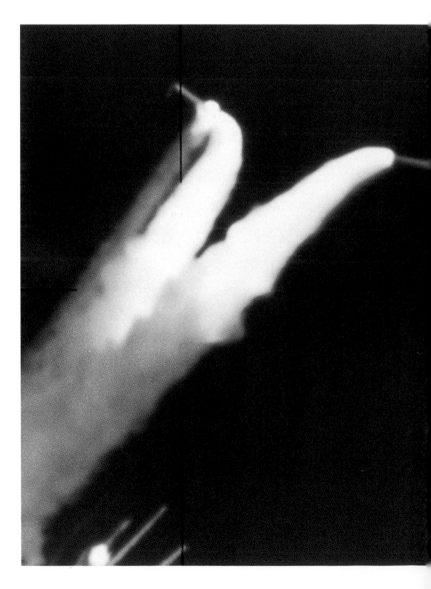

The final moments of *Challenger*, as 73 seconds after the launch, the shuttle explodes in a giant fireball.

The Missing Minutes

What had happened on board *Soyuz 11* between the last message from Commander Dobrovolsky and the silent landing in Kazakhstan? In Moscow, the capital of the **Soviet Union**, a special commission was set up to find out. Headed by Mstislav Keldysh, the President of the Soviet Union's Academy of Sciences, it began to talk to the experts responsible for the *Soyuz* mission.

Around the world experts on space travel tried to guess the cause of the disaster. Many thought that the heat shield that was meant to keep the **Command Module** cool as it plummeted back to Earth had failed. In Moscow people close to those who ran the *Soyuz* mission were saying that a hatch had not been closed. The air in the Command Module had leaked out, and the **cosmonauts** had died.

The *Soyuz 9* mission pictured here had a happy ending. However, when the *Soyuz 11* command module was opened up the deaths of the three crew members were discovered.

3   The eerie silence is worrying. But the parachutes and rockets designed to give the cosmonauts a soft landing all work perfectly. The Command Module lands on target in Kazakhstan. Doctors are first on the scene to check the health of the three men. But when they open the capsule they find the three men hanging from the seat straps. Somehow, during the 20 minute **re-entry** phase of the mission, the three men have died.

4   An official announcement from the Soviet authorities says simply '...a helicopter-borne recovery group, upon opening the hatch, found the *Soyuz 11* crew in their seats without any signs of life. The causes of the crew's death are being investigated.'

On the night of 27 January the temperature dropped. Unusually for Florida there was ice. Early in the morning engineers were out on the launch tower removing icicles. Behind the scenes at Mission Control there were arguments about whether or not to go ahead with the launch – the effects of the cold weather on the Shuttle were unknown. The predicted launch temperature of −1.7°C (29°F) was far below the coldest launch so far. But at 11.38am the launch went ahead anyway.

Challenger rose into the clear blue Florida sky. 50 seconds after launch the Shuttle broke the **sound barrier**, and continued to accelerate. Mission Control sent the expected signal, 'Challenger, go at throttle up'. 68 seconds into the flight the commander on *Challenger*, Dick Scobee, gave the response 'Roger, go at throttle up'. Seven seconds later *Challenger* exploded into a giant fireball.

> *'Obviously a major malfunction...the vehicle has exploded.'*
>
> Steve Nesbitt, a member of the Cape Canaveral control team, tracking the flight on a computer screen at Mission Control.

New Space Age

The first US Space Shuttle was launched on 9 April 1981. It was the world's first reusable spacecraft. The Shuttle could complete a mission in space, glide back to Earth for a runway landing, and be ready to fly again within 100 working days.

The Shuttle was designed as a reliable work-horse, ferrying **satellites**, people and materials into space.

Countdown to Disaster

As *Challenger* exploded there was a stunned silence at Cape Canaveral. Relatives were at the launch-site to watch the lift-off. As well as Commander Dick Scobee there were seven crew on *Challenger*. One was an ordinary teacher, Christa McAuliffe. She was on the Shuttle to give lessons from space. None of the crew survived.

This section of the Shuttle carries the **payload** and the crew members. It is designed to glide back to Earth at the end of the mission.

1   The cold temperature on 27 January causes concern about the **booster rockets**. At a meeting between **NASA** and Thiokol, the company which built the booster rockets, Thiokol engineers say they have no idea what effect the cold weather will have. One engineer, Roger Boisjoly, warns, '...success of previous flights should not be taken as proof of safety'. But the launch is allowed by NASA.

2   Lift-off at 11.38am. The temperature is very cold for Florida – much lower than at any previous launch.

O-rings

Challenger was carrying two **satellites** to put into **orbit** in its loadbay.

7 At 73.13 seconds after lift-off an explosion totally consumes *Challenger*.

6 By 65 seconds a bright glowing flame is burning on the side of the booster rocket. At 72 seconds *Challenger* itself begins to burn. It is at 13,800m and travelling at nearly twice the speed of sound.

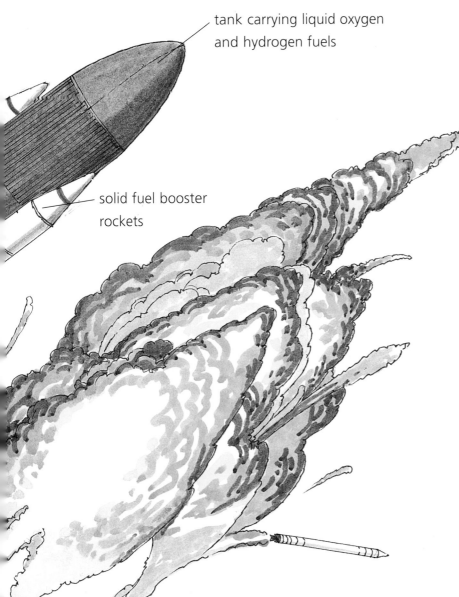

tank carrying liquid oxygen and hydrogen fuels

solid fuel booster rockets

5 At 59 seconds into the flight a fire begins to blaze. Pressure readings show that the right-hand tank is losing fuel fast. The flames are spreading.

4 37 seconds after lift-off high winds begin to batter *Challenger*. The weakened joints begin to leak again.

3 Within one second of the launch a puff of smoke appears from a joint in the right-hand booster rocket. After two and a half seconds seven more puffs of smoke appear. They are black, and it looks like the seal, called an O-ring, in the joint is burning. The burning rubber reseals the leaking joint.

23

The Fatal Mistake

After the *Challenger* disaster a Presidential Commission was set up to find out what went wrong. A fleet of recovery vessels used **sonar** to search the seabed for bits of the *Challenger*. Wreckage was dredged up. But little trace of the seven crew members was ever found.

The Presidential Commission made its report in June 1986. It pinpointed the cause of the explosion as the O-rings, which sealed sections of the solid **rocket boosters**. But it said the cause of the disaster was the decision made by **NASA** to launch *Challenger* that fateful day. NASA had gone ahead with the launch in spite of the cold weather, and in spite of warnings from engineers who believed that the O-rings were a problem.

The seven crew members who lost their lives when *Challenger* exploded.
Front left to right: Michael Smith, Francis (Dick) Scobee, Ronald McNair.
Back left to right: Ellison Onizuka, Christa McAuliffe, Gregory Jarvis, Judith Resnik.

O-rings

NASA investigations traced the cause of the explosion to simple rubber seals between the sections of booster rocket. These seals are called O-rings. In each joint there are two O-rings, each less than a centimetre thick. These seals were made stiff and hard by the cold weather. Instead of flexing and giving a good seal, they failed. Fuel escaped and burned, and *Challenger* exploded.

Rocket failures

Solid rocket boosters, similar to those on *Challenger*, had been used in nearly 2900 flights on the US space programme. 121 of these rockets had failed.

The Presidential Commission found that managers at NASA had taken too many risks. Dr Feyman of the Commission said at the enquiry that: 'The Shuttle flies with O-ring erosion and nothing happens. Then it is suggested, therefore, that the risk is no longer so high for the next flights. We can lower our standards a little bit because we got away with it last time. You got away with it but it shouldn't be done over and over again like that.'

There were no Shuttle launches for three years after the *Challenger* disaster. America had suffered a huge loss.

As part of the *Challenger* inquiry the O-rings on the future 61-G mission were checked.

The Space Race

Until a few years ago, people often spoke of the 'space race'. There were only really two runners in the space race – the **Soviet Union** and America. No other countries had the billions of pounds needed to design, build and launch space rockets.

The Soviet Union and America competed to be first – first into space,

An American astronaut carries out repairs on the Hubble Space Telescope. Until the Shuttle started flying it was nearly impossible to fix the complex and expensive **satellites** in orbit.

first to do a **spacewalk** and first to the Moon. Yet the costs of space exploration were, and are, huge. So there was always a conflict between the engineers and experts who built the space rockets, and the politicians who paid for them. The engineers and experts were cautious, and wanted to have plenty of time to test equipment to check it all worked perfectly. Of course, the politicians wanted equipment to work too, but most of all they wanted spectacular successes for their own countries, such as being the first to put a person on the Moon.

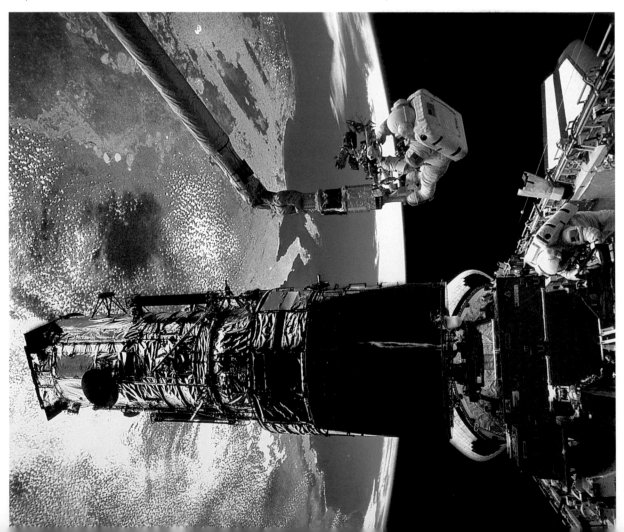

It is vital that all satellites are properly tested before they are used.

Most of the time the politicians got the success they wanted. And both the Soviet Union and America achieved incredible things. Yet sometimes the demand for new successes affected safety and cost lives. The *Challenger* disaster is one example. This was a very important flight for the American space programme. There were 15 more flights planned for that year. Any delay with *Challenger* would have caused problems for the rest of the year. The Shuttle programme also needed to prove that it was worth all the money it was costing. These pressures meant that when the weather turned cold, and the flight should have been cancelled, it was not.

The World's Worst Space Disasters

There have been 207 **manned** space flights. Fortunately, only a few have resulted in disaster.

Baikonur Cosmodrome, Kazakhstan, USSR, 24 October 1960
A rocket, preparing for launch, exploded on the ground killing 91 people.

Apollo 13, **April 13 1970** The US *Apollo 13* spacecraft was on route to the moon. 60 hours into the mission an explosion disabled the **Command Module** forcing the crew to abandon the mission. Fortunately *Apollo 13* made it home safely with the crew.

Soyuz 11, **29 June 1971** The **Soviets Union's** *Soyuz 11* spacecraft had spent 22 days in space. On **re-entry** into the Earth's **atmosphere** the Command Module lost pressure and the three **cosmonauts** on board were killed.

Challenger, **28 January 1986** Seven US astronauts were killed when the Space Shuttle *Challenger* exploded 73 seconds after launch.

This is an artist's impression of the explosion of oxygen tank number one on board *Apollo 13*. The crew never made it to the moon, but they got home safe.

Valentina Tereshkova was the first woman in sapce.

Space dangers

Each rocket and the spacecraft it carries contain many hundreds of thousands of separate pieces – from simple seals to complex computers. There are a huge number of things that could go wrong, and sometimes something does. It is almost impossible to build a back-up for every system, so the failure of one small part can destroy a whole mission. All of the disasters in this book were caused by small problems: *Apollo 13* was crippled because of the insulation on some simple wires; the crew of *Soyuz 11* died because of a single **valve**; *Challenger*

Record breakers

First person in space
Yuri Gagarin of the Soviet Union. In April 1961 he spent 108 minutes **orbiting** the Earth in a spacecraft called *Vostok 1*.

First woman in space
Valentina Tereshkova of the Soviet Union. She piloted the *Vostok 6* spacecraft in June 1963.

First people to land on the Moon
Neil Armstrong and Edwin 'Buzz' Aldrin. In July 1969 they landed the *Apollo 11* **Lunar Module** on the Moon.

Longest stay in space
Dr Valery Polyakov of the Soviet Union spent 438 days on the Russian space station *Mir*. He returned to Earth in March 1995.

blew up because of the failure of a seal just millimetres thick. Perhaps it is surprising that there have not been more disasters in space. But as long as there is space travel the dangers will always be there.

Glossary

air pressure the density of the gases in the air. We need a certain air pressure to be able to breathe properly.

altitude height of an object above the Earth's surface

atmosphere envelope of gases which surround the Earth, or a planet

booster rocket large extra rocket used to get the main spacecraft started off the ground

combustible capable of burning

Command Module part of the spacecraft where astronauts spend most of their time during a space flight

cosmonaut Russian name for someone who goes up into space

friction force created when one object moves across another

fuel cell cell making an electric current from a chemical reaction

fused melted together

GMT Greenwich Mean Time

gravitational pull force of gravity pulling objects towards each other

gravity force which attracts objects together and which holds us on the ground

jettisoned dumped or thrown away

launch pad platform with supports used to launch rockets into space

Lunar Module craft designed to travel down to and back from the Moon's surface

meteorite piece of rock from space

NASA National Aeronautics and Space Administration

orbit oval path through space around a planet or the Sun

Orbital Module part of the spacecraft where the astronauts live when in orbit

payload items carried on board the spacecraft, for instance satellites

pressure suit suit that protects an astronaut from space, supplying air and heat

pressurized when the inside of a craft is pumped full of air so the astronauts can breathe in the same way as they can on Earth

re-entry when a spacecraft re-enters Earth's atmosphere

retro-fire when engines burn to slow the spacecraft down, so that it does not go so fast that it burns up in the Earth's atmosphere

satellite object put into space to do tasks such as sending out telephone or television signals, or taking photographs of Earth and Space

Service module part of the spacecraft which carries important equipment

sonar way of finding objects by bouncing sound waves off them

sound barrier high resistance of air to objects moving at speeds similar to that of sound

Soviet Union Also known as the Union of Soviet Socialist Republics (USSR). This country no longer exists but split up in 1991.

space walk an astronaut leaves the spacecraft in a special suit

Teflon now used on the inside of saucepans, but it was first developed as a heat resistant material for use on spacecraft

thermostatic device that automatically controls the temperature of an object

vacuum where there is nothing; neither air nor gas nor water

valve device that controls the flow of gas or liquid

venting leaking gas out into space

weightless/weightlessness astronauts feel weightless because they cannot feel the effects of gravity in space as they do on Earth

Index